New Red Words

poems by

Larry D. Thacker

Finishing Line Press
Georgetown, Kentucky

New Red Words

Copyright © 2024 by Larry D. Thacker
ISBN 979-8-88838-801-3 First Edition
All rights reserved under International and Pan-American Copyright Conventions. No part of this book may be reproduced in any manner whatsoever without written permission from the publisher, except in the case of brief quotations embodied in critical articles and reviews.

Publisher: Leah Huete de Maines
Editor: Christen Kincaid
Cover Art: Created by author and Microsoft Create AI
Author Photo: Larry D. Thacker
Cover Design: Elizabeth Maines McCleavy

Order online: www.finishinglinepress.com
also available on amazon.com

Author inquiries and mail orders:
Finishing Line Press
PO Box 1626
Georgetown, Kentucky 40324
USA

Contents

Preface—2024
Star Epiphany 1
I Question Mars on A Late Spring Night 2
Mars Mission—Crew VIII. Humanities Personnel. 2031 3
A Mars Proposition 5
Someone asked, What in the world.. 6
The One-Way Show... 7
Last Days on Earth, Easier Than I Figured 9
Mars Weather Report? 10
The Bells.. 11
Superior 12
Trans-Mortem History 13
Over-planeting... 14
The Earth Once Spun Faster Than This 16
Ours... 19
There are no mile markers in space. 20
Results Varied 21
She read my palms in zero gravity. 22
Anti-Gravity... 23
Alternative Transportation to Mars 24
Looking out at the black. 25
Planetary Juxtapositioning 29
Poet's Mission #1 Accomplished 30
Entreaties 31
The Mars Poet Walks the Sands.. 32
A Martian Sends an Email Home.. 33
A New Poem 34
Homo Sapiens Fossilis (Cro Magnon Type) 35
Disorder in a Far Dark.. 36
What to expect in a new town. 37
"Mission to Mars"—1959 38
Novelist suffers writers block on Mars.. 39
Poem-A-Sol on Mars... 41
Colonial Boot Hill Established: 2031 42
Crater Ridge Canticle.. 43
After First Blush... 44

Coprotes Montes: Map Feature ID 15326 45
To Then Share a New Red Name 46
Missing Water 47
Yes, It Snows on Mars 48
Renaming on Mars 49
Must we label the space 50
Father Randolf 52
I worry a little 53
Eight of Wands 54
Feather: A Color Study after Ted Hughes 55
Nursery Rhyme for the First Born 56
Where It All Gathers 57
Pareidolia #1 58
Soul Retrieval 59
Noise 60
Home Waters 61
This isn't *Star Trek* 62
Whole-Harbored 63
When you're thirsty, look to the horizon, ... 66
Thou Wilt Likely Covet on Mars 67
Unfortunate 68
Off the Shoulder of Orion 69
So. 70
Mars Field Notes 71
Sandstorms are more like stone storms. 73
Three Found Poems on Mars 74
On Assignment 75
Dream Disease on Mars 78
You're alone. 79
Erasure 80
Why wonder the truth on such matters? 81
Holding fast to your Earth details, ... 82
Mammoths on Mars 83
Writing 84
Back Around 85

Preface—2024

Humanity is headed to Mars. This one brave act changes everything, lending a duality to our daydreams, de-familiarizing our night gazes up into the dark with our children, newly shading our mistaken beliefs on the simple color red. Those first arriving will shoulder the scientific burdens, preparing the paths of pain, experimenting in physics, geology, engineering, health, AI, robotics. But the humanities must follow on, for we will not simply visit Mars, we are going there to live, to die. To remain will mean to thrive in a world of the word. The ground, the rocks of the planet, will demand a poetry of their own, and every art, as quickly as the first imprint of a toe pressing the soil. The planet waits for new red words. So very patiently.

I

Star Epiphany

What is it besides mid-autumn's impending cold
that so invites the gathering of wood, the building of fires?

What about a season's first nose-full of campfire
ignites that ancient memory of cave huddling?

What deeply seeded shift wakes us near the center,
tempts us tiptoeing away from firelight and warmth,

from the safety of others in the middle of a clear night
to stare up at clouds of stars with a new wonder?

**I Question Mars
On A Late Spring Night**

Air waves vibrate
your most visible night,
so close, a mere
forty-six-point-eight-million
miles from our little spot,
give or take a block,

cruising in traffic, rainy night
smearing the windshield world
in doubled streaks that bleed
and correct in light speed beats.

I glance up into parting
clouds lit like a dying fire
by city street life,
but it's all the same,

brakes, intersections, turn signals,
head lights illuminating stop signs.

With this many markers, I wonder,
will we ever make it to you?

Mars Mission—Crew VIII. Humanities Personnel. 2031.

The scientists and engineers and physicians went out first,
all NASA-nauts, super-competitors, fame-bound from birth
probably, perfect health, perfect teeth and hair, pedigrees,
the 4.5 minute miler geniuses who could research, build,
problem solve and survive for what was left of their lives
on their new inhospitable home of the Mars World Project.

With enough of those sorts, they were called a colony.

Rumor has it how one of the first scientific crew sent word
after her first year on planet:

>> *There is no poetry here* <<

Those who knew, knew better, of course. If there were
eyes and ears and lips and tongues, minds and fingers,
beating hearts, there on the planet, poetry existed.
But who would create this strange new language?

There was a call for a one-way-trip historian, teacher,
songwriter, artist, novelist, and yes, even a red planet poet.

Critics were ruthless. A television show based on how zero
gravity effected creativity and the mind, with dozens
of artists crammed into a satellite commune for a year,
with two voted off each week with the help of the audience,
only lasted a single season. It was a terrible plan.

The experts took over.

It morphed too bureaucratic, of course, with calls
for applications and corporatized mission statements:

Q: *Why do you want to write poems on Mars?*
A: *Who could resist but to write poetry for Mars?*

Crew VIII, specific to Humanities Personnel, responded
to that strange one sentence cry for help. And that's what
we knew it to be, we humanities experts, we "touchy-feely

thinkers" as we were known, the underfunded storytellers, we cave painters, we stump-sitting philosophers to be shot into the stars to ruminate on the what ifs of rocks and sand.

But more than anything to venture past the world of the binary, though all our static umbilical lives are linked in 0s and 1s, to find the in-between world, to give sociologists and anthropologists more than mathematics to wonder on, to offer posterity so much more than:

>> *Sol 1: Sunrise: 7:37—Unremarkable* <<

A Mars Proposition

After Maggie Nelson's Bluets

Let's suppose I'd simply gotten tired
of being here. Suppose I'd believed

that gave me options. Let's then say
I'd have left out years ago if I could

have. The more unfriendly the science
made Mars sound to human survival,

the more I craved being there, thriving
in even lonelier atmospheres. Suppose

I'd have signed the dotted line willingly
in as much of my earth-enriched blood

as you required. Might this have gotten
me here to there any faster, I wonder?

Someone asked, What in the world

will you write about? It hadn't struck me yet,
how immediate the vacuum of physical material
would be. They acted as if we'd be cut away,
untethered from news from the world
in which they remained. But no,
we'll be as informed as anyone, delayed
only by the speed of light. It makes me wonder
what the shrinking blue dot might sound like:
whether gunfire and protest chants
and debate rhetoric and deodorant commercials
and burning buildings and the *tap, tap*
of thumbs on cell phone screens can change.

What's the first thing I'll miss, as the Gs hug
my body into the seat and a tiny star's worth of fuel
burns behind us like a maddened comet?

Worry. I've been getting up early and watching
the news, staring into the morning sky,
like a good political junkie should, driven

by questions of what happens next?
But the higher we shoot into the sky,
as the world shrinks and vanishes to a pinpoint,
the tinier those headlines will become,
the less noise they'll generate.

Elections? Prison terms? Starvation?
Hollywood tantrums? Statues yanked down?
The restroom enigma? Covid-26?

Are we supposed to just forget?
Yes. Don't look back, I'm told:

"For wherever two or more find themselves,
there wilt thou be blessed with the news of the day."

The One-Way Show

I imagine the museum as a one-way ticket, twilight
falling outside happening only once, space moving
in as I make way through the revolving doors
and refuse to glimpse back.
                       They say you can't look
back to the ground once the countdown commences.
The room full of reds is the only hall I'm visiting,
barely noticing anything else along the way,
Rothko's own special color pooled in a spot,
blocked to clouds, planet forming in there it seems
and never letting go.
                     When one shade on shade would
blur to blinding after staring too long, like horizons
I'd soon face and wonder on, I turned, again,
again, through the night, another red view waiting,
like rock and dust yet introduced to eye and word.

>>>>>>>>>>>>>>>>>>>>>>>>>>>>>>>>>>>>>>>

I dreamed of Arizona wind for four months.
It's where we trained. In the Yuma Dunes
and the Mojave Desert, out in Death Valley,
and in the puzzles of New Mexican canyons.

I carried some sensual hope into the blankness
of space and dreams my memory of the scent
of Arizonan rock, growing accustomed to the idea
I'd never stand on a high rock's outcropping

at sol's sunrise or sunset, inhaling a full chest
of genuine Mars atmosphere, unless behind
the sterile glare of shatterproof Plexi-glass.

>>>>>>>>>>>>>>>>>>>>>>>>>>>>>>>>>>>>>>>

Rothko would admire the tones here,
washed out as they are on most days,
but caught just right at both twilights.
And the odd mix of turquoise and blue,

small transitional worlds between red
sand and rock, one becoming the other,
an eternal grinding of wind and missing
water, where a brush blurs boundaries.

Last Days on Earth, Easier Than I Figured

Last few days in the old college office,
lounging for a moment, not quite verging
on nostalgia,
                not just yet. But it won't take much.

Window open and feet up. The crack of a bat
and ball, shouts of urgency, my breath merging
in wind. Vision flashing back from the evening
window glass. An exhaled thought tossed
away last spring,
                coming through again

having made its thousand circuits of the world
and gotten homesick and wanting back in
through the same window.

And what have you learned, out there
in the swirl of worlds: the politics of screaming,
of gunning engines through crowds, of fire-
bombing, the names of bully towns, how
to lock school rooms from the inside-out.

Inhale and give in some healing.
                            Inhale.

Clacking of cleats in fine gravel, red dust caught
and carried over the greening field, mown stripes.

Another bat cracking its echo over the lawn.

                I've got it, a kid shouts.

        No. I've got it this time.

Mars Weather Report?

I grew up
in the only town
in the country
in a meteorite crater.
The basin stretched
more than two miles,
the crater over
300-million years old.
On a topo-map,
you can clearly see it,
dipping in the mountains
like some gigantic
thump print of a god.
I would spin in our yard
as a kid, trying to keep
my eyes on the ridges
surrounding town
as I got dizzier.
I worried secretly
that if it rained too long
it would all fill with water
like the Great Flood.
My Sunday school
teachers we're good
at their jobs. It worried
me I'd never met
any ark builders in town.
When I was able
to put on my CV
"Grew up in meteorite crater,"
they thought it was
a joke until the interview.
No, it's true, I said.
As long as no floods
are forecasted,
I'll be right at home
where we're headed.

The Bells

I was finishing up a last lecture on campus
before heading back to base for a final weekend
of training. These were my last few hours

on campus, a home for years, and the bell tower
chimed every fifteen minutes over conversation,
like a passing moon, a reminder of a thing unique

for us all, as a class, as individual students,
for my leaving town, campus, and soon, Earth.
Where I was going would bells ever knell over

the red plains? Had I taken them for granted,
a simple thing among a million simple things?
Even with my feet steadied, gravity firmed,

on a quiet day in the trees on my farm later,
packing up, cattle lowing, the occasional clang
around their necks saying, here, here, no, here,

a gentling wind in the spruces, feet bare
on the sponge needles, out in the trees
where no red is seen, at least I knew some

bell calls somewhere by some hand, some
catechism upright through the air over towns,
somewhere a clanging, over and over, then

just dissipating before reaching me along
over the earth's forever curvature. I do not
hear it, cannot, but it always rings out there.

Superior

We build a fire tonight,
like others will.

Not only to cast up our smoke words
to commune in some special way
with this so-called super moon,

but that we might mingle
our home fires with others
just here along the surface

of this super planet, where
we're taught anything is possible
for the right reason,
including building fires
to a wild rock in brightened orbit

to feel a little closer
to some we ought to love
a little more.

Trans-Mortem History

Will anyone be around
to dig on our analog bones,
let alone wonder what stories,
poems, family portraits, selfies,
and cat poses, once circulated
the lost electricity of flash-drives,
the lasered grooves of CDs,
the internal binary hard drives of laptops
or server-filled rooms, fully
cobwebbed now, moldy
with roof leaks, the echoes
of what preoccupied
the neuro-electrical pulses
inhabiting our minds, when once
we only cared what shade of ochre to swish
in mouths and spit-spray over
our sprawled hands along
carefully chosen cave walls?

Over-planeting

This is the closest to death we'll come, being alive,
our untethering from any remaining purposes
with the earth-bound, unbound soon, shipped up
to the new off-land, we're ghosted into darkness,
       by choice, necessity.

So, we learn a new embrace
      for the first, last time,
those you'll never touch again, but only speak with
echoed: with *real-time*, at best, a three-minute delay,
forever, your hugs, impressed in photograph,

   or as skin memory.

But I was almost too careful as to who
I spent time with those last days, no matter
how intimately I trusted them, or how familiar
the history of a book or trinket they carried.
  After all, we breathe a memory of the past
in molecules, in redistributed energy.
        In echo.

In every gasp of excitement, fright or worry,
we invite nano-castaways: from a desert turned glass,
or from the repeated shouts of "Hands-up!
Don't shoot" or "Incoming!"
  or "Get under your desks! Hurry, kids!"

I didn't want to carry off an ill wandering ash,
some nightmarish elements
from a madman's executed plans,
a hint of genocide tucked somewhere in the gut,
and transported safely through the black.

Yet we have the touch of last kisses
       inhaled and held so deeply
in the lobes of lungs, greedy and airtight, transported
like another life, a fire, carried within, hibernating,

never exhaled fully, cooped up in life pods and suits,
willing to wait the necessary seasons
                            to seed a new world.

The Earth Once Spun Faster Than This

Much faster. Too fast for life. But it slowed.
Enough for just the right stuff to hang around
long enough to settle in and set up the shop.

But it's a perpetual slowing, though, say those
in the know, assuring guaranteed comeuppance
for blameless generations yet dreamed up

by those killing themselves and us so slowly
now and yesterday. When it comes to rotation,
too much is too much, not enough is not enough.

One flings you off, the other floats you away.

In either case, it's nothing but space and time
for anyone remaining in the shop at the last,
left to tumble along in the dark with this rock.

II

Ours

Our noiseless ambition floating now,
        there is no turning back in this space,
        no changing plans, though minds, bodies,
        and spirit are rendered vulnerable, we spin
        up some gravity of bone and muscle redemption
        along the edges of the craft, hoping.

Our merging trajectory set,
        we all spacewalk a magnificent razor's edge
        of destruction, willingly,
        in constant irradiation, ignoring
        the inner vibration of wreckage we'll not feel
        until it's too late perhaps.

Our new lightness awaits, a little less
        of ourselves, unburdened
        of an entire world's weight behind us,
        yet shouldering all of being's being
        for the deathly chance to step into the red.

There are no mile markers in space.

Nothing is sufficiently still.
No matter how thrust is perfectly timed,

the gentleness of robotic release,
all is flung from the original Great Center,

dark matter carrying all things invisibly.

All in sleep. All in waking. Entire
galaxies drifting intact, the same

gravity biding what keeps the atoms
of your clenched hand convinced

it's a hand in your traveling sleep,
your eye an eye during those long blinks.

Cast out something from yourself:
A quiet opinion, a glance, a muttering,

some sacrificed prayer to the vacuum,
see how it races to keep up with you,

mirrors your trajectory, like a pet echo.

So, calm yourself. You'll know
you're there when you get there.

Results Varied

Sleep, they instructed. Sleep.
I remember wanting to dream.

Wanting something to write about,
as a writer, of course. They said
results varied, so I left a pad and pen
Velcro-d securely to my side bar.

Don't puke on it when you're revived,
the tech advised with a laugh,
searching out a good arm vein.

Revived—what a term.

We slept for two weeks at a time
then would live normal routines
for three weeks.

Little coma vacations, I think
the tech called them as he slid the tube
down my throat.

As everything went fuzzy.

Everyone gets sick,
but not everyone dreams.

She read my palms in zero gravity.

Recognized valleys etched along my flesh
we would soon walk like sand seas, mapped
from overhead like from a single good eye.

Traced one hand's marks, then the other,
sought out any mirroring still latched
to either since before my birthing, strained

to see future funnels in whorls of storms
on three planeting fingertips, the dark
freckle on my left palm, in the dead center

of my fate line, an oval of missing light
where a perishing star once sighed its last.
I was born with a strangely deep lifeline,

she reported, confused that it wasn't long.
All the more reason to leave the old planet,
I figured, closing both my storied hands.

Anti-Gravity

Breathless grunts of a newborn,
half frustration, half amazement,
neither remembered by old age.

That ill-definable desire
for things unreachable
as a pristine, invalid,
alien child: a floating

in wonderment. Orbiting hearts.

When we are in the midst
of this stage of being, can we feel
any literal root in the old stardust,
as newly gathered swirling?

Galaxy of our own astonishment.

Alternative Transportation to Mars

I would have
wanted to go anyway,
chosen or not.
I would have
ciphered some manner
of finding my way
back to my mother's womb,
sent strange future / past
words back, convincing
enough for her to choose
to birth me there in the cold street
of the inter-world
trip lottery lines,
among the waiting
thousands.
I would have waited then,
grown up there
on that avenue,
called it mine, called it place,
called it home, learned
what things I needed
or not, watched
the street lights
and the stars, the one planet
flashing red and swinging
by for those years
until the lucky time came
for me to go,
some way, somehow.
Poet or not,
I would have
been on my way.

Looking out at the black.

What do we see?
After the echo—
and let's agree
echo is a terrible word
for such a mystery
persisting—
fades, finally.
We might call it
a quickened memory,
mostly unmoving,
though prettily streaking,
perhaps, as if a portion
of this thing,
has some desire within
to escape.
      Knows
it's dissipating there
in the sudden closing
off. And it does
in that instant.
And a kind of darkness,
but more akin
to a cousin to dark
comes along.
A twilight
behind the eyes,
let's call it.
And let's agree
the lids of our eyes
control
      everything,
closing down over
all movement and sound.
A killing filter.
Leaving only
a danger of imagination.

III

Planetary Juxtapositioning

*You don't miss that mysterious scent
of water, everywhere, until never seeing
a lake, or stream, or mud puddle again.*
                Graffiti on Mars living quarters pod wall

It's blue there. So very green.
All things reflective in water.
Black in rich soil. Tan in sand.

It's colorless to a blackness here,
until pecked in echoes of dead
and dying stars, in hints of others
born in destruction, their dust
and planets, in light-devouring
lightless wells.
                It's all those shades
of red you've been expecting,
but butterscotch, too. Creamy
butterscotch dunes, so deadly.

Streaked browns, the burnish
crater rims, the swept tan flats.

The bluest sunrises and sunsets.
Rose skies the rest of your days.
Everything you dreamed. More.

Poet's Mission #1 Accomplished

There was a package in my waiting gear.
Nothing I'd brought along, but a care box
of items stored in my quarters for my arrival.
A tiny, plain tin canister, space-sealed:

to be opened after the poet's arrival,
after some comfort is found in the new life.

How long would that be? Months later,
having grown too curious about the riddle,
the time came one night. I hadn't shaken it,
put my ear to the cold tin, like a kid
on Christmas morning. I unscrewed
the stainless-steel top away, revealing
a few scoops of settled ashy stardust,
and a small shaky handwritten note:

I think my spaceship knows which way to go…*
If you'll only take me outside for a little waltz

We shared some tea that night, played
music, and I'm afraid I talked to myself
a bit more than I'd like to admit, humming
songs I'd not thought of in a million miles.

I wouldn't dare scatter the ashes myself.
I'd let the planet have the honors.

Securing the can, lidless, atop a rock cairn,
the coming night wind and crystal view
of the Milky Way would do what it would
by morning, but not before I dabbed
my finger and tasted the dust, before
walking away, greedy for a little last
communion before the sun gave out.

*David Bowie—"Space Oddity"

Entreaties

Someone fashioned a space efficient altar
in a corner of Common Pod 2. Sacrificed

a little table space for what we can all use
as a friendly communal spot to remind us

we're all in this together. Simply. We can
put what we want there. It was crowded

when I got here. A Ganesh statue. Rosary.
A cairn of tiny stones. A piece of twisted

debris from 2029. Saint Cupertino's icon.
A short string of faded prayer flags above.

The Book of Mormon. Incense we'll never
burn. Gold and silver candles. A hammer

etched of silver. A post-humanist's guide.
A mason jar, set out on the flats for a year

collecting starlight. I dip my fingers in it,
make the sign of the cross. Whisper, *Amen*.

The Mars Poet Walks the Sands

When might they send a priest, we asked once,
curious as to the Colony's plans. A holy man
or woman? What sort is needed? What brand
name of common shaman? What sacred scrolls
have you found in the caves of Tempe Terra,
have you dug up amazing shrines in the sands
at Syrtis Major Planum?

                Or are you newly baptized
by some Martian Messiah hidden away for eons
in the cave pits waiting for disciples to arrive?
But, are you not your own shamanic priesthoods,
confidants, witches, healers, speakers-of-tongues,
living out your own slowly rusting martyrdoms?

Send someone into the wilderness
                            to find who waits.

I wandered out there, knowing no bushes waited,
only long-ago bubbled lava rocks, no manna
floating among the twisters, and crunched up
my suited body into a lotus position and rested
by a shade ledge, staring down an old dry Wadi,

                waiting out the spirit
of God to move again across the face of the sands,
an envisioned flash flood prophesied that if
one would sit and wait, with stones and songs,
a tsunami of riverous epiphany would answer
in half-sleep, full of stars and space tumble,
a returning echo from some muttered prayer
sent up and out on a last breath, eons ago.

A Martian Sends an Email Home

after Craig Raine

\>> Shiva is the conversion system used for producing
oxygen from the planet's rich carbon dioxide atmosphere. <<

\>> A storm of sands is a ghost-wheel of civilizations past
rolling on soft ground in frustration, leaving no trails, but
wanting to be noticed. Wailing as the wind anyway. <<

\>> She was here before us.
We burn scarlet incense on the ridges. <<

\>> The F-6 tornado is when there is no such thing as windows
here in the pods for fear of pressure failure. No chances are taken.
All is witnessed through electric screens and a shatter-proofing. <<

\>> She halts the great walls of sand that would take us.
The twisters that would dance on our heads for our deaths. <<

\>> Rovers pressurize to save our lives, let us slide
into new skins from inside, live inner-worldly,
seeking to strike rocks with our third and fourth arms,
second skulls, twice-legged. <<

\>> Scrawling new Sumerian scratches
over the dunes for satellites to wonder on
after we've held breaths and turned a truer red. <<

A New Poem

I wrote a poem today. Rune-toed it in the south dunes
as best I could with my big cumbersome boot.

A Mars haiku:

> The rocks are thirsty.
> The sands are like ice water.
> The valley throat is empty.
> The stones are not fooled.

I didn't want to write it down and bring it with me,
glad the thought would be taken up soon by the twisters.

But so far out here, where everything reaching for life
deserves a story, the rhythm stayed with me like a mantra,
stepping with me on my morning hike along the crater rim,
and by the time I was back I was ready to write it down.

Something had changed between out there and the pods.
I'd carried in only its essence with the dust of my boots,
a thing struggling for life now, with or without me.

It wasn't the same poem. Couldn't be. And I struggled
to call up the words, never sure if a first version
of memory comes close enough to the truth.

A Mars haiku:

> The stones remember.
> Even the days of water.
> Even the dust on my boots
> Cries out for a drink.

Homo Sapiens Fossilis (Cro Magnon Type)

Kept in Le Musee de L'Homme, Paris

There is a skull in Paris, rust stained and rough worn,
in the earth once as it waited the tools of archeologists,

and when inspected closely now appears Mars like,
perfectly so, bringing to mind our mutual mortality

and the one-way slow suicide everyone criticizes.
But is it really such a death, leaving a planet already

determined to doom itself? It seems pre-destined.
Like the graceful first to be honored in red dust,

bound to alien ground and slow covered in burial,
a newly interred spirit dwelling among the rocks,

all of us, red skulled too, given enough new time.

Disorder in a Far Dark

Just calm down. Don't panic.
It's a colonial cliché. *Relax.*
Have you tried meditation yet?
It really does work anywhere
in the solar system, you know.
She's not that convincing.
You are still on your meds?
You know what is convincing,
though? These millions of miles
from my old security blankets?
How a false heart attack feels.
How easily you're convinced
this is the one. Finally. Or, if not,
how the idea of crawling back
into a completely safe skin suit
causes something strange to happen
in your brain. Or waking up
having forgotten how to breathe,
as if your O2 gave up on you
out there down in a crater. Alone.
It's a singular horror that nothing—
no doc or meds—ever fully gets.
If things were a little better,
what would that look like?
Can you describe that feeling?
Yes, I say. It's as if dying here
would be fine. As if the planet
itself wasn't out to kill us all.

What to expect in a new town.

Keep meeting the same 238 villagers
turning the low-ceilinged corners
every sol, moods revealed in florescence,

the air's scent combined strangely
of everyone's odor, faint of red sand,
through overworked oxygen scrubbers.

The same few decks of playing cards
turning thin as antique book paper
along the corners. The canteen meatloaf

resembling nothing like your mother's
past the first year. Your lone walks
along the far crater rims lasting

a little longer each time you go out.

"Mission to Mars"—1959

> *"Through telescopes, astronomers have seen large, green patches on Mars that spread widely during Mars' summer season, then fade to brown during winter."*
> "Mission to Mars"
> *Space Travel Golden Stamp Book*, 1959

They say the grass is greener.
Or is it down the road in another
neighborhood, with a gated fence?

Or across the road, where the promise
of a better chicken coop awaits,
constructed to order, personalized
with a fancy monogramed letter
on the wrought-iron screen door?

Or out a few more million miles
down some monumental metaphoric road
where Mars blushes in potential importance.

And that's it, really: the *greener* inquiry.
Unknowable potential.

A fine enough question to ask,
with hope, optimism, in an era of limited answers.

In a simpler day, when green
was green, and the future
was ever and ever brighter.

Novelist suffers writers block on Mars

I

Paces from the bed to the window. Again.
Sees the same blue-tinted sunset, whip

of beige dust, tracked up red dirt. Closes
her eyes again, tighter. Opens them. Sees

swimming stars swirling, their fading. Tries
eclipsing the memories of home interfering

with any story arcs living here. Here before
here knew us, here after here is rid of us.

Paces from the darkening window, the self
reflection, to the desk, the too quiet space.

Protected by so thin a thought just outside,
from the driving dust, the great killing cold.

And inside: Life circulates the florescence.
A plot writes itself one dangerous decision

at a time, here, which is the hook, she thinks.
What doesn't kill you, makes you Martian.

II

What are you going to write about
when you run out of things to write about, son?
my father asked. It was a good question.

You sure do write a lot about trees and hills,
those rivers you head out to when you can't think.
I'll have the internet, I told him, laughing
at my own absurd answer. *And virtual systems,*
of course. Son, you were always the first
to smell the ocean when we went on vacation,
remember? When we were miles from the beaches.

He was right. *You'd sniff out the salt air
before anyone. And as a kid you warned everyone
of the snowstorm moving in because you swore
you could smell it? No one believed you.
Remember?* I did remember. It did snow.

For three days. I thought I'd discovered magic.
There won't be much of that there, huh?
He was right. *It'll smell like tracked in rust,
I suppose. Maybe that's what I'll write about
when I run out of things to write about then.
The memory of coastal salt in the air.
That scent. And you, here, reminding me.*

Poem-A-Sol on Mars

You learn to find prompts in gradation: stone size,
sand up to boulders, all the in-betweens, guessing
comet and asteroid size, meteorite speed before

impacts. Or maybe how many novel shades you
might find, and words created, for *that thing.* You

determine, as an exercise, to utilize only new words
for that dominate color that *should not be spoken*
by virtue of its majority holding on all things present:

beginning with alizarin, a favorite tone, you recall,
of one Bob Ross, and commence categorizing what
forms of happy little alizarin copses of trees might

magically come into being on the hills by morning.

Colonial Boot Hill Established: 2031

Captain Jerald Smithers was buried on a gravel hill
three-hundred meters off from the pods and over
a berm of sand and rocks that always reminded him

of his native southern Arizona near Tombstone.
As the first to pass on the planet, and lucky enough
to see it coming, everyone agreed he should nickname

the cemetery what he wanted. His family visited
the old west town when he was little. He'd run along
the rows of dead, kicking up the rough sand, wild

as a desert horse, fascinated with the hand-painted
grave signs and their crazy stories of shootouts
and murders in a new land where your days were

hard won victories. He was there when I arrived,
in the ground. That's all he wanted, they say. A good
hand-painted sign about dying with his boots on.

Crater Ridge Canticle

> *"I seem to have come to the end of something, but don't know what"*
> Charles Wright—"Last Supper"

It's so much reversed, turned inside out, upside down,
New-fangled and bettered, strapped to a longshot holding our breath,
A new sub-species:
                  sand wolves howling at tiny, oval tumbling moons.

To chase anything here is to chase ourselves.
For every discovery of a new thing reiterates the hunt, sets
Into merged motion the same cycle of purpose, pushes

The planet over for yet another sol,
                  yet another day for exhaling new names.

After First Blush

When did a first allotment of words
for colors fall short, first disappoint
with insufficiencies requiring new
nomenclatures of light and dark shades?

What was this history: after simple red
turned scarlet resulting from some
incident concerning blood, or when it
conspired with rain to birth rusts,
or with snow to soften into rose.

And what of blue? What peppered it
lightly enough to a powder or enriched
the sky to just fine a point so we might
finally evolve eyes to see azure? What

of this silly competition by paint makers?
Their industrialized epithets, graded
at micronic shades to complement couches,
bathroom throw rugs, and bed comforters
for newlyweds or new college freshmen,
never getting the color match just right,

after insisting on eyeing it, guessing over
handfuls of samples, only to find that colors
fade and the names change every season.

Coprotes Montes: Map Feature ID 15326

After Han Shan

It is said the Coprates Mountain Range is odd.
That researchers come back from work spooked,
Haunted by what they've seen while digging ice
Under the stars in the deep and darkest valleys.

Shadows echo too long there, turning to voices,
Reminding quickly of those left forever back home.
The exposed ice glistens like so many lost eyes,
Searching for voices dancing through the valley.

To Then Share a New Red Name

I watch the rest of the artisans venture out.
The stone carver. The novelist. The soprano.
All toiling on their greatest works.

The painter is out this evening in the deep
caves off to the north of the craters,
mixing some dark manner of found tint
to smear over the walls of her stone canvass.

She and the playwright are in collaboration.
They insist their first completed work must
preempt the first native of the planet, a child
soon born we're told, and after reaching
an age known by them, this chosen one
must discover the cave paintings, bringing
an end to this finely orchestrated performance.

Only then shall the child and colony be named.

Missing Water

A dark matter lived
deep, past the once beach,

the salt spray of the past
is a taste in the nose

and on the tongue, a constant
voluminous roar, decaying

to skeletal forgiveness,
roaring back tidal, sands up

the river basin, soil
shifting at some quantum

level, specks revolving,
one-for-one, peripheral loss

of sight, sphere shift
under dark mattered lives,

rolling back heavy,
mythically-placed

and volcanic voiced,
bubble rocks rolling

in the once surf, tidal,
oceanic, over-journeying.

Yes, It Snows on Mars

Efi misses fall, and used to rake up leaves
and run and jump into piles with her son
when he was little. Samuel told me he misses
coffee shops; mostly the soft din of dialogue
rather than the coffee, and Alfredo worried
who he'd talk to without his pet crow.

As for me, it was snow I'd miss most.
I was in a training class, and it had snowed
all night, a finely powdered snow, crunchy
under the steps, half-a-foot of it, every limb
tufted white, little drifts everywhere.
How could I not miss this most?

But it does snow here, but differently,
as dry ice, the atmosphere's carbon dioxide
super frozen. I've yet to see it.
I'm like a young native Floridian
whose only heard rumors of it happening
somewhere else on the planet, seen pictures
and footage of it on a screen.

Our living pods sit on a lightly buried glacier.
Ancient ice, bands of old fallen snow
waiting to be sipped by us as excavated water.
I want to go out there and dig.
Past the sandy crust of the lava tube,
tunnel my way to it all and scrape at it
gently enough to make snow,

hold it high in my hands,
let the wind lift it away.

Renaming on Mars

How long before we morph
words? What awaits newly the eyes
deserving monikers of their own?

Will an alphabet spring naturally
from sand and rocks, the heated
and frozen air? Might some
new script system simply slide
off our tongues one morning

in the midst of a normal conversation
over breakfast about the day's agenda?

Samples research and poetry prompts
suddenly mixed with sounds
especially resonant in oxygenated
chambers or vacuumed helmets
and pressurized suits, syntax given up,
eyes focused in special purpose,

a planet silenced of its secrets.

Must we label the space

in between as the dark: dark
matter full of dark energy,
dark days adding into dark ages?
Things feared: dark
shadow, dark under the bed,
in the hall through the crack
of the door, a scratch
at the window after dark, shift
in the closet's dense infinity.

Alone: alone, as in floating
so far out in space, away
from planets and stars, no craft,
naked, with only a mix of live
and dead starlight reaching in
from the multi-trillion cloudy blinks.
In such a first, truest absence
of proximal light, in this
aloneness, would we see
our own hand in front of our faces?

Between one memory and another
are dimming flashes of holding on.
The fading starlight
billions of years culminate.

There, forever, but not: *Gone.*

Light: existing for a time,
now only points along the in-between,
not made dark,
                     made in darkness.

Even light is an arrival
of particles, craving solidity
upon which to breathe.
Points of light as smaller points,
perpetual energy refusing destruction,

found another time, perhaps,
in some other state:

unlit. Alone, but never fully dark.

Father Randolf

traversed more than space to get closer
to his god: *That Which Hears All Things.*

It was his one-way trip into a prayer
he claims will never end. A priest,
self-stranded on a planet with a moon
you never see, that he's named *Amen.*

A rock in constant eclipse.
A mathematical impossibility, yet,
there it is, the lit ring rolling the night sky,
as if it hiding from its own being,
an all-seeing eye, collapsed
on its own questions.
                              Closed.

I asked him if coming all this way
felt a little closer. He reminded me
there is no up in the vast amazement
of space, no north. Only out. *Ever Out.*

I worry a little

that the more I mess around
in my outdoor environment suit,
the better chance there is
I'll break a pressure seal,
or some other deadly accident.
Three-million dollars
gets you an engineer's suit,
not a poet's for wandering
the dunes and rock hills
chasing your ghost muse.
It's built for the slow,
meticulous sort of work.
Procedural: Problem.
Bolt. Nut. Hardware choice.
Mechanical movement
of the body, dancing
with the broken machine
that must be up and running
to continue keeping you alive.
But again, I want to skip rocks—
nice, perfectly flat ones,
from this ancient riverbed—
as hard as I can out against
that mirage so tricking the eyes,
like fresh water. All the while
knowing this suit isn't designed
for such work.

Eight of Wands

The governments couldn't keep a psychic away.
One would eventually wander space and touch down,
hidden under the guise of an ice miner or botanist.

Frieda was Wiccan. Frieda was a physician.
A seventh daughter of a seventh daughter. Born
in the tall Kentucky hills. Trained by a granny-woman

in centuries-old folklore before she ever considered
heading up to the university in Lexington. To cure
and to know was what rushed in her born-in blood,

and when she told her mama and papa she would
escape those isolating mountains one day,
where they shot her cross-wayed looks of distrust,

no one believed her until she was already learning
how to shuffle her Tarot deck in zero gravity.

Feather: A Color Study after Ted Hughes

Black is the space between your eyes
and the 100-billionth exploding star,
black is the throat wheeling upon itself
searching out words and their sounds,
so also is the night's skull just as black
as snow would never be, cannot be,

black is the soil, black are the graves,
hidden below the mile of iced ancientness,
the core shot up and black, straight
through to the blue turning to black,
beyond earth's atmosphere, into the quiet
raging black with no fear or heartache.

Red is the taste of our mouths, mashed
in on themselves, self-loathing the absence
of blood, red the taste of missing limbs,
of black bird wings, and other blackened
things, red grow the eyes too far set back
in the mind, red too are the danger thoughts,

fired and mystified in the darkest rooms,
the lightless rooms of red turned black,
red the name of war, the killing, conflict,
naming itself black but knowing it is red.
Red is the black of the sky, high enough
to forget itself, forever red, forever black.

Nursery Rhyme for the First Born

A tooth lost on earth, another lost in space,
And one lost on mars, all from the same face.

One red rock. A black rock. Some blue and blood.
A smooth black river stone screaming from above.

Sand ground underfoot, minced by locked jaws.
Formed into a plaster, etched deep with scroll law.

Sunup and sundown, each sol seems the same.
Buried ice from north and south bares no name.

A bone in a limb is marrowless still, while
bodies from a blue planet are sleeping on the hill.

Knick, knock. Tick, tock. Whatever shall we do,
with all this extra time since we've landed on you?

Where It All Gathers

There's a body of water in my thoughts,
a kind of hodge-podge of tributaries

forked together over dreams or real places
passed and seen, waded into, not fully river

or creek, or an ocean. Whatever it is, or
where it originates singly, it all merges

eventually in the center dip of a pasture,
under a copse of safe cedars, a denseness

I must crawl through following the call
of waters skipping and finding a rhythm

before a moment of pooling and swirl.
I watch there as light gathers from nothing,

the waters spinning, pulled into the planet.

Pareidolia #1

Anna, an environmental artist, is completing a new work.
An anonymous New York donor commissioned the piece.

She's been out working on the installation for over a year,
using overburden from the ice mines and tunneling

to construct a hilltop half-a-mile long and almost as wide,
leaving long trenches giving the appearance from above

of eyes and a mouth and a nose. With a decent enough
telescope, it should be visible from Earth. But an annual

dust storm is whipping up in the northwest, threatening
to cover up Anna's work. The donor doesn't really care

this will happen, as long as it's completed before the storm
hits in two weeks. The auction is already scheduled.

Soul Retrieval

When Michael Collins snapped his photo
of the descending lunar lander in 1969, Earth

was in the background and he was the only human
in any form throughout time, living or dead,
not in the shot.
                    I thought about that photo when
we all gathered up for our first colony photo.

How Ray Alders, our post photographer,
was repeating the Collins shot in his own way,
insisting on standing out up on a rock
rather than using a timer and joining
the other eight-point-eight billion of us,

Earth as a rising white twinkling speck
just on the horizon, rising over our heads
and over our little city of life pods.

Noise

Joli said that after spending a year
in the Utah desert pods she'd been cured
of needing the sound of a thunderstorm playing
to fall asleep. That the sound she'd grown addicted to
was the constant snipping of sand grains
against the plexiglass portals of the pods.
That this was oddly just as soothing to her
in those moments of drifting off.
That the similarities of impacting water droplets
and sizeable grains of sandy dust weren't much
of a stretch to imagine. That as long as she could see
the dust storm lightning on Mars
through her closed lids she'd know
the dream was holding on.

Home Waters

There was an old town fountain my grandfather loved
to visit when I was a boy, an artesian well flowing
since before he was a young man, the fountain's sides
slickened with a red accumulation that fascinated me.

He'd lift me. I'd strain to touch my lips to the crystal arch
of cold water tinged with that odd rusty taste I'd learned
to associate with our trips to town.

                    Now that chemistry
is a constancy in the mouth, iron oxide along the gums,
that bloody dust a hint of red horizon on the tongue,
a rust world at every turn in the air and on the words,
attempts at sterilization a constant, but incapable
of washing memory from taste.

                    The waters back on Home One
leaden heavier with grief, and plastics, heavy metals.
With politics. How did we manage to get out here
when we're so obviously doomed there? Resources.

The lusty sub-surface promise to binge,
                            surely. So, before
the droves arrive to gorge and drink up this island's ice,
let us fashion some fountains here for our few young,
bottle up this red oasis of quiet purity for a little time.

This isn't *Star Trek*.

But it's not Earth, either.
Remember back in 2031,
when the first crew got here
and stayed? Were we all
heading to work in flying cars
every morning, taking meetings
by holodeck, or transplanting
brains into better bodies?
More than ten years on now
and we hear how much
smarter phones have gotten.
That driverless car fatalities
are increasing. That VD
is down thanks to AI elbowing
into the sex industry. But here,
we're existing in living pods
hardly better than cargo crates,
hunkered down again
under another sandstorm,
and rationing water
until the engineers fix
the filter units. It's like falling
behind from the future.
I've been playing solitaire
with a smuggled deck
that's quickly rotting away.

Whole-Harbored

Anchor-worn, dark strung drug
from the gut or to a lobe of the mind,
it's full harvest, waterless
and rust welded,
                        out in limb sacrifice,
transplanted. Transmuted.

Warm. Dead cold. Warming.

Replaced with a fuel for light
in some other state,
                        or country,
or full horizon. World-flattened.
Tossed into one of a thousand
craters of contemplation.

>>>>>>>>>>

        Docking: I'm at a tearoom
in Asheville, North Carolina,
lounging shoeless and prone
on a century-old Persian carpet,
back against pillows, head resting
on a girl's lap.
                    She whispers:
I'll never see you again: Drink.
Feeds me her Rooibos in deep red sips,
from her mouth, pushing away
my hands. They float to my sides.
My legs are light, my feet buoyed.

>>>>>>>>>>

Our only tidal drift is pulsed sleep here.
Sub-worlds with every closing of the eyes,
going under, sipping
the lost light, soundless, adrift
in stone shift and blush waters,
rose wines for drinking

in all the what ifs? Baptized
in cliché, yet on the new what?

      Call it: planet, sphere, danger river.

>>>>>>>>>>

This morning's sunrise.
Blue, with an inner light rising,
all over red, the blacking above.

Rothko's "Number 61 (1953)"

>>>>>>>>>>

The researchers try
their strange new math
in low gravity, find
they haven't the words
for how a single soul
etched all this erosion, before
eroding itself to trudged rune dust,
never stilled, dry heated
into canyons, crater storied.

>>>>>>>>>>

We take nothing for granted in this light.
What creeps behind in long shadow.

Has God caught up to us, or bothered
noticing a smallest portion on the scales
having shifted,
             or checked back lately at all?

Maybe God sends postcards
by way of life killing comets,
objects hurled into space a billion years ago
harboring great tidings, if only

for a few seconds of brilliant epiphany.

>>>>>>>>>>

      Undocking: I walked out
of that tearoom in the mountains
imagining licking the blue and red rocks

where I was headed, where thirst
promised to kill unless miracles
were in place.
                I hesitated, listening
for what music the lingering taste of lips
and tea might mix up in my belly,

lion, wildebeest, and zebra
tracking through me in herds,
searching out summer watering holes.

Driven by thirsts born to them

                before their making.

When you're thirsty, look to the horizon,

scan the evening's haze for the pale blue
of resentment, for the tiny glints only your home

water sphere speaks, salty in sparkle, veined
in fresh rivers, the cool embrace of clouds

as only a memory. Think on how you once
stood, ankle deep in the shoreline, looking

for the wink of this red planet as a child,
wondering if another little boy, just like you,

was staring back across the quiet ocean,
a rush of blanketing dread washing over

when you both realized how holding
your breath for too long brought visions.

Thou Wilt Likely Covet on Mars

How long do you have to be here
before you accumulate enough junk
to warrant having a yard sale?

Does anyone remember when the next
Saturday might be? And are flyers
necessary, or will word of mouth suffice?

Not that there's any money to exchange
when even breathing's bartered,
but there are things coveted, surely.

A slice of something similar to what
peanut butter pie might taste like, traded
for an extra working ballpoint pen.

Some dry macaroni art of a snowman
for three back massages upon request.

Or a million hectares of quiet desert
for your last pack of American Spirit.

Unfortunate

I've wondered how long it takes a Mars stone
to roll itself into nothing but red sand? Might
this be every stone's ultimate desire? A release.
If it is, it's a shame some aren't able, trapped
in some geological trick of nature, while winds,
textures here are perfectly made for grinding
everything to an eventual sandy nature.

Yet add water and we have the earth mystery
of the sliding rocks along Racetrack Playa flats
in Death Valley. Single rock streak imprints
surrounded by dried, cracked mud, as if these
stones lived, were inching their way across
the desert when no one is looking, searching.

But someone always eventually seeks and finds.

Did winds push the rocks over rain-slicked mud?
No. It's something else. When the rains collect
in the ancient lake and freeze, but begin to melt,
panels of ice detach and float, striking lone stones,
sliding them, digging in trails of muddy mystery.

Should we lament a stone's missed opportunity?
Born on the wrong planet at the wrong time?
Suffering some bad karma, perhaps? Born into
a wrong family? These rocks will never enjoy
the chance to tumble and roll, to collide, shatter,
rub down, shrink smaller over eons. Not knowing
what they don't know, they are doomed to slide
calmly, willed along by the moodiness of ice.

*Off the Shoulder of Orion**

I've slept in the caves of Alamar Crater
when lightning pregnant storms of dust

cut the sun off for weeks. When counting
breaths and reaching blindly for food,

napping between transmissions, was how
we spent our lives. I've gone two days

without coming in for resupply to watch
a few hours of rare Fata Morgana mirages

along the poles. I watched helpless from
millions of miles as earth fought its fires

in the west, nothing magnificent in them
to discover but the assurance no trees wait

here for the ignorant. Only space for planting.

*Quote from Roy Batty, replicant,
"Tears in rain" monologue, *Blade Runner* (1982)

So.

It only takes the idea of a few unaccounted-for pounds to keep rocket engineers and investors up late at night, so, it's almost unheard of for anyone to possess books. I mean, a real, hardcopy book. Not something you can access over microwaves from a bottomless pit of data, but a tangible, in-the-hand book. I was allotted, as poet, a mere fifteen pounds of "literary material." For a time, I owned the only non-Earth library in the solar system. Until the most unexpected soft knock at my panel door signaled the quiet rebellion that not even a bureaucracy of life-and-death physics could hold at bay. The visitor stood there with a copy of Seamus Heaney's translation of *Beowulf*, a tiny, light paperback issue, no weightier than a newborn bird. *Hide this*, the new stranger asked, near begging. *Don't worry yourself*, I assured the man, we've not been here long enough to start burning books. And besides, there can be no such thing as fire on Mars.

Mars Field Notes

I.

When I got the word I'd be leaving
I more or less abandoned the farm.
Those last spring weeks I quit mowing
the field, left long stretches of the yard
to their own fallow wishes. Watched.

It takes no time for earth to reclaim itself.
Just a little laziness on our part, a little
forgetfulness. My excuse for sitting it out
on my 100-year-old wrap-around porch
observing the grass and weeds compete
while my bottomless bourbon glass sweated,
was a practiced permanent absenteeism.
I was already long gone. The old place
deserved to know something was afoot.

II.

It may be all packed rusty dirt and rock,
some loose dust, but it's hard not to wonder
what else once stood where I'm standing:
last week, last millennium, last eon, last forever.
Things have ways of vanishing given enough
patience, water, heat, pressure and wind.
No studied imagination brings a life back.

III.

The farmhouse back home must be a wreck
after four years, the foundation weakening,
windows cracked, roof leaks finding way
into the inside walls, rotting things
from inside-out. I know the kudzu creeps
closer every spring, dies off by winter
without recoiling, leaving dried woven vines
everywhere it wandered, a hard layer

of carpet over the last year's network,
eventually decomposing to enough weight
to collapse the second floor, to pancake
it all into splintered humus, slow equal toned
as acid rains steal color all winter
under the growing hills of what looks like
only a large puzzle of roadside weeds.
When will a hint of my ever being there
be fully gone? Am I to be excavated?

IV.

How long does it take: weeds to soil,
soil to clay, clay to ground, ground
to dust, dust to sand, sand to powder?

"Remember you are dust,
and to dust you shall return."

If all things can fraction down to no thing,
who might be caught off that red mesa
past the craters, coming in tossed winds,
inhaled: Who do I harbor then, back
to the pods each trip out and in, no longer
myself, stowaways no longer lost?

Sandstorms are more like stone storms.

The light off our continuous beacons
spins and the storm debris flies
as if there's not enough gravity
out there to pull all the sand and grit
to the ground, just a few feet more.

It appears as if we're back out there
and flying through the black again,
through an asteroid field, every speck lit,
and like out there a harmless gravel
bouncing across our hull, every impact,
is a tiny constant wiggle of turbulence.

Every strike a potential deadly missile.

I think back on all the old movies,
like *Star Wars*, when lights streak back
as ships dashed out into light speed.
Would this resemble reality if we catch up
with our imaginations:
                              A window's
side view of space rushing by, reminding
some of us of stretching out in the backseat
of our parent's car, flying down the road,
the streetlights and windows of houses
flashing in lines of colored light, quicker
and quicker as our father's accelerated.

Three Found Poems on Mars

A pebble, knuckle-sized, beige to **pink** in the sun,
        resting as if placed in the popped bubble of old **lava**
A palm of bluish sand **poured** slow over a smooth stone
            while imagining you're **the planet**'s sole hourglass
To think that most of what you do might be a first in the universe
A **bore** hole through a stone sends a bolt of **light** to the ground,
        traveling only a few inches this time of season, and if
        the **sands** here happen to not shift on that ground,
        will that spot of sand lightly **fade** over a million years?
The crunch of salt **crystal** under boots in the morning
I **dreamed** of kudzu last night. **Long valleys** of relentless,
        luscious planet **covered in** kudzu.
        A long scent of warm green.
The **incessant red** that never grows old
Mistaking the black hole light at the center of the Milky Way
        night for the sun
Running across your own boot tracks over **time**
        and considering them a sign of **crowding**
I woke up **craving** bacon this morning and realized it was
        over 100 million miles away, too far to bother just for bacon
The soil here looks leached away like the **clay ground**
        around my family graveyard where they strip mined
        leaving only the graves **and a single tree**, an island of irony
There are **no fortune** cookies on Mars. You must bring your own.
        Cookies. And fortune.

On Assignment

> *"And after the commanded journey, what?*
> *Nothing magnificent, nothing unknown.*
> *A gazing out from far away, alone."*
> Seamus Heaney—"Lightenings"

I.
You can't not write about what you'd like to
run from. There's no artistic ex-patriation
from the fray, especially at this ridiculous distance.

Especially since we're never going back.
You can't outrun what threatens you at home.
Elections, water, air. Worldwide depressions.
Wars, disease, lacking resources. Specifically:
mystery plagues, electronic combat, autonomous
drones, new military states, internet hacking wars,
the US Constitutional Convention of 2033.

We brought all this with us.
They send it to us, like a radio wave
poison, with every communication.
It's in there. Always in the staticky background.

You thought you were escaping? The epitome
of collective escape even. I daresay not,
they write of you and what you're being here
means of them, and what their still being there
means of you, and await my interpretation
of it all in universal metaphor. It's just an exchange
of headlines: danger and politics and gossip.

If anything, we're loaded here with the past,
both presents—here and there, mirrored—
and a contracted future we report on with each
beat of our still working hearts. And, of course,

there's no running from here: it's all exposure
past the craters. No readership that we've found.

II.
Better to write of what's remembered,
un-murdered by the hands of catastrophe,
spared by the hands of we few on this future.

Being here, you miss the simplest of sounds:
a crow, a tree limb squeaking, the skitter
of little unseen things above and below.

The barn door creaking closed, the baby's coo,
a hotel desk bell over street traffic,
a train horn and a fire truck all at once.

The garbled whoosh of party conversation
after you've gone under water, the chorused
gallop of a hundred frightened desert horses.

III.
Tell the ones back home we're getting on
as good as them. The usual ups and downs,
a few broken bones, some broken hearts.
But we mend faster with the low gravity.
That's to our advantage in a new civilization.
They can't expect us to be just like them.
After all, they get all that oxygen with so little
effort and we get what? A few extra minutes
on every day and all this adventurous attention.
How's that for an even trade? Not bad.

IV.
We see the *Curiosity III* rover out there.
Sometimes a meandering blip
on the proximity screens, rolling half-blind
over the flats, smacking headlong
into rock formations before righting.

From a few vantage points, like
how Death Valley low dives and dips,
you can see an eternity, how the clouds

so easily doubled in shadow like black ships
over the sand, that's when I've seen her.
Her shine is worn to a deadened patina,
harder to pinpoint. I watch for her dust tail
kick up, like a smoke message. She reports
a jumble of digitized photos, corrupted
by the storms, the lightning strike,
forever our wandering unreliable narrator.

Dream Disease on Mars

We circle up to meet at least once a week now.
Amber's distressed. She talks about forgetting

how to dream. That these empty white walls
and repeated meals and same suits of armor

are robbing her of anything new to process
in her sleep. That the longer we're all gone

from Home One, the less she can recollect.
The assembly leader reminds, she is home.

Amber goes silent. We try talking about how
to make new memories worth inviting up

to sleep's threshold. Even dragging material
into the dreamscape if necessary. For becoming

fully dreamless here, we've agreed, is a death.

You're alone.

You absolutely know
you're alone out here.

But you know you're not.

Like when you claimed
you didn't believe in ghosts,
but did just enough, down
where it counts,
that when you felt that
shift of awareness
you didn't second guess it.

And now it happens again.

And you look around, moving
your whole body since
these helmets hide the periphery.

Back on earth they used to say:
You don't know what you don't know.
But here, it's more like,
you can't see what you can't see.

That movement reminds you
of how you did the same
back home, even without a suit,
in that old house
where you tried, but failed,
spending the entire night.

Erasure

The mightiest forests are the potato and bean crops,
singularly lush, under controlled flickering suns.
They thrive under three nightlights, lit in a way

I imagine as stationary moons. The only rivers here
stream from tin cups to our thirsts, or in tiny rivulets
along precious harvested soils emptied of poisons.

The grand lakes are frozen and buried by the sands.
The winds, being a thing we see, but never touch,
are rather the moving of air in whispers, lips to ears,

or across the countable leaves in the rooms of green.
We have one bonsai, brought as a two-inch tree,
now a lovely six-inches tall. Jamie sometimes

dreads trimming and shaping it, but she keeps on.
To not do what is necessary alters a thing forever.

Why wonder the truth on such matters?

Who knows what this ball of rockish dust must be,
spinning, orbit-axised, seeming un-kept in correct

in-motioned velocity and distance from our home
sphere of compacted elements; soil and water

and magma and flesh and lust and warheads
and malls and Instagram filters and dirty socks—

chunked off and slow-rounded, items tossed
from our world? *Earth*, as we've named ourselves.

Or is this moon, his keeper of tides, some
gravitationally immerged body of partially destroyed

and particulated, pulverized meteors, asteroids,
comet ice, tugged and knitted like space quilts

by some out godly wisdom we shouldn't want
to know, who hides in its unknowable self

what such a mystery ball of rockish dust, spinning
and axised, so perfectly and oddly kept, must be.

Holding fast to your Earth details,

insisting on writing about *back then*,
is a way of suicide on this planet,
but to somehow forget about it all,
will be just as obliterating to the self.

You're in a bind here. A purgatory
of choices. It's taken us some time
to figure it out. I've thought of home,

and hurt. I've killed off memories
and hurt. I've floated in the middle
and hurt. There is no hidden spot here

that doesn't demand its word sacrifice.

Mammoths on Mars

You bring us here to de-extinct?
Here of all places, where everything

is experimentation. Humankind
must have been becoming very lonely.

Perhaps it is fitting, breathing now
this recycled air, created as we have been,

somewhat cruelly re-animated
where none of our ancestors roamed.

Where should be go when we feel death
pacing behind us. Where, when none

of the old graveyards of our memory
can be found without trudging space?

At least we're not alone, here with you,
in the red deserts, where everything

is leveled a day from extinction. Together,
doomed on a journey of second chances.

Writing

each entry is like a last transmission:
a tiny hidden goodbye

somewhere buried in the dunes
of narratives,

even if it's not personal, and most
things here aren't personal,

it's all us and we,
the old-world pronoun

relegated to a lowercase priority,
re-incarnated to appear,

oddly enough, as if a small being
with a round helmet:

an individual.

Back Around

It's a kind of momentary amazement,
fleeting, but lingering long enough
to be convinced you've crossed here

in this hesitation, that this might be
yet another swing through, another
take, another edit, not another trick

of the writer's constant mind. Fiction
maker's head? It's faded and gone
before you can analyze it by much

and you've almost forgotten it all
by the middle of the day, but frames
flash in by mid-day, bringing doubt,

but most importantly, and here's a
a strange thing, it mostly leaves you
with the faintest feeling: in the end,

everything is going to be just fine.

ACKNOWLEDGMENTS

Mars Mission—Crew VIII. Humanities Personnel. 2031.	*Ghost City Press*, Oct 2016
A Mars Proposition	*Avant Appalachia*, Dec 2017
Mars Weather Report?	*Avant Appalachia*, Dec 2017
The Bells	*Burning Water*, Dec 2016
Trans-Mortem History	*The Wild Word*, Feb 2017
Anti-Gravity	Mockingheart Review, Nov 2016
Entreaties	*Hollow*, Broken Tooth Press, 2016
The Mars Poet Walks the Sands	*Arcturus Magazine*, Nov 2016
Disorder in a Far Dark	*Deaf Poets Society*, Crips in Space 2017
Poem-A-Day on Mars	*Free Lit Magazine*, Nov 2017
Crater Ridge Canticle	*Avant Appalachia Zine*, Dec 2016
I worry a little	*Riverbabble*, June 2017
Nursery Rhyme for the First Born	*Arcturus Magazine*, Nov 2016
Planetary Juxtapositioning	*Eyedrum Periodically*, Jan 2018
Renaming on Mars	*Eyedrum Periodically*, Jan 2018
You're alone.	*Eyedrum Periodically*, Jan 2018
When you're thirsty, look to the horizon,	*Ink & Nebula*, 2018
A Martian Sends an Email Home	*Electric Athenaeum,* "For Future Generations" Issue 2018
Over-Planeting	*Red Planet Magazine*, Nov 2019

Larry D. Thacker is a Kentuckian writer, artist, and educator hailing from Johnson City, Tennessee, where he lives with his wife Karin. His poetry and fiction can be found in over 200 publications and is widely anthologized. His books of poetry include five full collections, *Drifting in Awe, Grave Robber Confessional, Feasts of Evasion, Gateless Menagerie,* and *New Red Words,* as well as two poetry chapbooks, *Voice Hunting* and *Memory Train.* His fiction includes four short story collections, *Working it Off in Labor County, Labor Days, Labor Nights: More Stories, Everyday, Monsters* (co-writer with CM Chapman), and *The Wicked Road to Yam Junction* (forthcoming), as well as a fiction chapbook, *Lemon Street's Angel of Death.* He also wrote the popular folk history, *Mountain Mysteries: The Mystic Traditions of Appalachia.*

Thacker has multiple degrees, including a B.A. in History, the M.Ed. in Counseling and Guidance, the Ed.S. in Higher Education Administration (all Lincoln Memorial University) and the MFA in creative writing (West Virginia Wesleyan College). A veteran of the US Army, Thacker served in the intelligence corps as a linguist / interrogator. He teaches English part-time for East Tennessee State University and Northeast State Community College. He was a regular cast member on the popular Netflix show *Swap Shop,* a vintage hunting show set in East Tennessee. Visit his website at: www.larrydthacker.com

www.ingramcontent.com/pod-product-compliance
Lightning Source LLC
Chambersburg PA
CBHW020338170426
43200CB00006B/424